MESOPOTAMIA

Christine Mayfield, M.S.
and Kristine M. Quinn, M.S.

PUBLISHING CREDITS

Content Consultant
Blane Conklin, Ph.D.

Associate Editor
Christina Hill, M.A.

Assistant Editor
Torrey Maloof

Editorial Assistants
Deborah Buchanan
Kathryn R. Kiley
Judy Tan

Editorial Director
Emily R. Smith, M.A.Ed.

Editor-in-Chief
Sharon Coan, M.S.Ed.

Editorial Manager
Gisela Lee, M.A.

Creative Director
Lee Aucoin

Cover Designer
Lesley Palmer

Designers
Deb Brown
Zac Calbert
Amy Couch
Robin Erickson
Neri Garcia

Publisher
Rachelle Cracchiolo, M.S.Ed.

Teacher Created Materials
5301 Oceanus Drive
Huntington Beach, CA 92649-1030
http://www.tcmpub.com
ISBN 978-0-7439-0440-7

TABLE OF CONTENTS

ANCIENT MESO-WHAT?

People today are really lucky the ancient Mesopotamians (mehs-uh-puh-TAY-mee-uhnz) lived so many years ago. These people invented items that we still use today. They created the wheel and glass. They were the first to use coins and mathematics. They used an alphabet and calendars. They farmed and used **irrigation** (ir-ruh-GAY-shuhn) to water their crops.

◄ Creating interesting figures was common during this time.

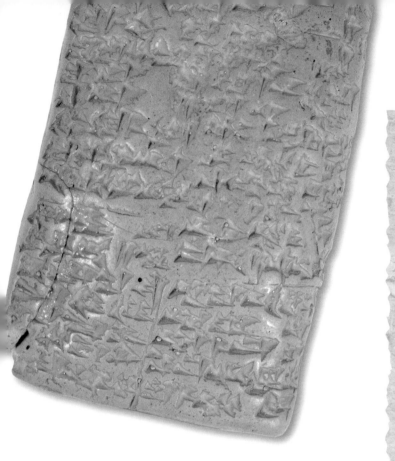

◀ This tablet shows ancient writing.

Amazing Mathematicians

The Babylonians lived in ancient Mesopotamia. They invented the decimal system, something that is still used today. They recorded the first calendar in which they divided the year into weeks. They were also the first to divide the days into hours, minutes, and seconds.

The World Today

How do you use the things created by the Mesopotamians in your life today? Imagine one day without these things in your life. The ancient **civilizations** (siv-uh-luh-ZAY-shuhnz) are still very important to us. We can learn about our lives by learning about theirs.

The ancient Mesopotamians were very artistic people. They decorated temples and palaces with strange creatures. The artists sometimes made creatures with both human and animal qualities. These might look funny to us, but the ancient Mesopotamians thought they were beautiful. Some of the creatures were symbols of greatness and strength. These qualities were very important to leaders in ancient Mesopotamia.

IT'S A SMALL WORLD

Ancient Mesopotamia was in the Middle East. Today, the countries of Turkey, Syria (SEAR-ee-uh), Iran, and Iraq are located there. If you want to find Mesopotamia on a map, you need to look for the country of Iraq. Then, find the Tigris (TIE-gruhs) and Euphrates (you-FRAY-teez) rivers. There you will find where ancient Mesopotamia was.

People lived in Mesopotamia as much as 7,000 years ago. One of the first cities was Sumer (SUE-muhr). Sumer was called a **city-state**. That means it was a city that ruled itself.

Later, there were other important empires that controlled the area. The empires of Babylonia (bab-uh-LOW-nyuh), Assyria (uh-SEAR-ee-uh), and Persia (PURR-zhuh) all controlled ancient Mesopotamia. Each city-state or empire had an amazing history.

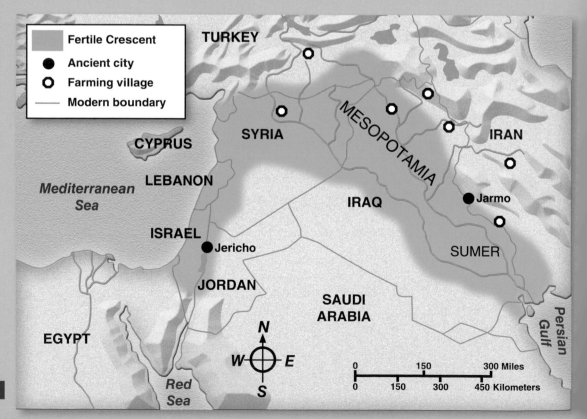

- **Fertile Crescent**
- ● **Ancient city**
- ○ **Farming village**
- — **Modern boundary**

TURKEY
CYPRUS
SYRIA
LEBANON
Mediterranean Sea
MESOPOTAMIA
IRAN
IRAQ
Jarmo
ISRAEL
Jericho
SUMER
JORDAN
SAUDI ARABIA
EGYPT
Persian Gulf
Red Sea

N
W ⊕ E
S

| 0 | | 150 | | 300 Miles |
| 0 | 150 | 300 | 450 Kilometers |

▲ These Iraqi children live in a violent land.

A Land of War

The country of Iraq is experiencing conflict among the people who live there. Other countries have become involved in the war. Many people around the world have been affected by the fighting.

Modern Development

Much of this land has been developed. There are major cities with large buildings and roads for traveling. Oil is a major product of the region.

▼ Oil refinery

THE FERTILE CRESCENT, OR IS IT?

Most of the ancient Middle East had a desert climate. That means it was dry and hot. However, there was one area known as the Fertile Crescent (FUHR-tuhl KRES-uhnt). The Fertile Crescent included Mesopotamia. Mesopotamia was the name given to the land closest to the Tigris and Euphrates rivers.

Everyone wanted to live in the Fertile Crescent. The soil was very rich. So, crops grew well. The people liked living near the water. The rivers allowed the people to easily get water for their crops. They could also use the rivers to move and trade goods.

Each year the Tigris and Euphrates rivers flooded Mesopotamia. After each flood, the area was left with rich **silt**. Silt was good for farming.

Soon many people came to live in the Fertile Crescent. Then, groups began to fight over the land because they could not live together peacefully.

▼ The Tigris River today

Controlling Nature

The Tigris and Euphrates flooded every year. By building **levees** and irrigation **canals**, the people controlled the rivers. These systems are still used all over the world today. They help move water from one place to another. You probably have irrigation systems near your home.

Not So Fertile Anymore

Scientists now know that much of this area is drying up because of the way people controlled the rivers. This is not good for the area. When people try to control nature, it can have a negative effect in the end.

▼ Wheat grew in the Fertile Crescent.

SUMER: ROCKING THE CRADLE

▲ Scribes were important in many different ancient civilizations.

Ancient Mesopotamia consisted of several city-states. Sumer was the first one to be recorded in history. It is here that one of the first civilizations started. This area is known as the "cradle of civilization." The earliest written records date back to around 3300 B.C.

The Sumerians (sue-MER-ee-uhnz) were among the first to put their language into writing. They used their writing to keep important records.

They first wrote in simple pictures. Soon the writing developed into a style called **cuneiform** (kyou-NEE-uh-form). Cuneiform was made with wedge-shaped symbols. They were made on wet clay tablets with a **stylus** (STY-luhs). Historians read the cuneiform to learn about daily life in Mesopotamia.

Cuneiform tablets ▶

Time to Go
to School

In some parts of the Middle East today, both boys and girls are allowed to go to school. But, they are separated. Boys and girls have their own classrooms. They go out to recess separately and play their own sports. Imagine going to this kind of school!

Back then, only some men could write. They were called **scribes**. Scribes were important and respected. Some boys attended special schools for 12 years to become scribes.

Writing with Pictures

The first writing was picture writing. The scribes used one picture to represent an object or an idea. Picture writing and cuneiform writing were difficult to learn. These are very different from our writing, which uses an alphabet. The Sumerians did not use an alphabet.

LEVELED SOCIETY

The Sumerian society consisted of some wealthy people. But, the majority of the people were very poor. They worked for the king.

Sumerian jobs included merchants, farmers, cattlemen, and fishermen. People were also architects, scribes, and artisans (AWR-tuh-zuhnz). Because so many items were created, Sumeria became a great trade center.

Men appointed by the king made sure that the trading was fair. They told the king if people were trying to cheat or steal property. Another important job was being part of the army.

▼   This piece of art shows many roles in Sumerian society.

Inventions, Inventions

The Sumerians invented the plow and the wheel. They were busy people. These two inventions have had a major impact on the development of **societies**. These items allowed for improvements in farming and transportation. Both are still important to people today.

Beginning Builders

There were not many trees in the desert. So the Sumerians had to use what was available to make buildings. They were the first to make mud bricks. They used these bricks to build temples to their gods. The special temples were called **ziggurats** (ZIG-uh-rats).

▼ Ziggurat ruins still stand today.

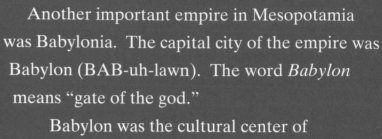

Babylonia: The Center of Culture

Another important empire in Mesopotamia was Babylonia. The capital city of the empire was Babylon (BAB-uh-lawn). The word *Babylon* means "gate of the god."

Babylon was the cultural center of Mesopotamia. Walls surrounded the city. There were many religious temples and beautiful palaces.

King Hammurabi (ham-muh-RAW-bee) ruled there. Hammurabi conquered the many city-states in Mesopotamia to create one large empire. He improved the irrigation system by keeping it clean. He also made the tax system and government housing better.

One of the greatest things Hammurabi did was to write laws. The laws were called the Code of Hammurabi. The Code explained crimes and their punishments. It also described legal procedures and property rights. The Code explained how to get loans, make deposits, and pay back debts. Hammurabi also described women's rights and treatment of the poor in the Code.

◀ The Code of Hammurabi

Read All About It

The Code of Hammurabi was carved on an eight-foot (2.4-m) black stone monument. The large stone was placed in the middle of town for all to read. It was one of the first documents about citizen's rights.

The People's Court

Hammurabi's political contributions are still seen today. They include an organized court system with judges. He had separate departments of government that reported directly back to him.

▲ The Hanging Gardens of Babylon are one of the Seven Wonders of the Ancient World.

BABYLONIAN RELIGION

◀ Ziggurats were tall so that the gods could easily visit them.

Religion was an important part of daily life. One of the king's duties was to serve as a high priest. The priests were important people who advised the king. The Babylonians believed there were many gods and goddesses who ruled the earth, heavens, and the underworld. The Babylonians were the first to study **astronomy** (uh-STRAW-nuh-mee), or the stars. They did this in hopes of getting messages from the gods.

Babylonians believed that a certain god or goddess ruled each city. This god or goddess visited the city's ziggurat. Ziggurats were similar to pyramids. The base level was the largest. The further up the ziggurat, the smaller the levels became. These temples were located in the center of each city. Only priests were allowed to go inside.

The Life of a God

The gods were thought to be like humans. They had feasts and wars. They even married and had children. They showed many emotions such as jealousy, anger, and joy.

Religious Roots

Three of the world's major religions started in Mesopotamia. The Christian, Jewish, and Islam faiths all find their history in ancient Mesopotamia.

ASSYRIA: BRUTAL FIGHTERS

Assyria was another powerful empire in this region. Its capital was Nineveh (NIN-uh-vuh). The history of this place includes many years of battles with other lands. The Assyrians (uh-SEAR-ee-uhnz) were known to be fierce warriors. They treated the people that they conquered very poorly. Their main purpose was to extend the Assyrian Empire.

Like other empires and city-states, the Assyrian king was head of the army. Many of the Assyrian people were soldiers. Other jobs included farmers and merchants. They were also scribes, artisans, moneylenders, poets, and musicians.

One of the most powerful kings was Tiglath-Pileser I (TIG-lath pih-LEE-zuhr). He is sometimes called the founder of the Assyrian Empire. He ruled from 1115 to 1077 B.C. Tiglath-Pileser was known for his military skills. He attacked Asia Minor, North Syria, Armenia (AWR-MEE-nee-uh), and Babylonia. He rebuilt temples and palaces. After he died, Assyria declined.

◀ Ruins at Nineveh

▲ This creature guarded the gates of an Assyrian city.

Quiet in the Library, Please

One of the first libraries was in Nineveh. It was built by an Assyrian king, Ashurbanipal (aw-suhr-BAW-nuh-pawl). It included some of the most important documents from the ancient world. Thanks to Ashurbanipal, we can read these works today.

Assyria Today

The nation of Assyria today does not exist. However, there are millions of people in the world who call themselves Assyrians. They live in Iraq, Iran, Syria, and Turkey.

▼ This relief shows an Assyrian banquet.

PERSIA: CULTURAL TOLERANCE

The Persian Empire was the largest in Mesopotamia from 539–330 B.C. The empire reached from Egypt to India. The capital was Persepolis (purr-SEP-uh-lis).

One of Persia's greatest kings was Cyrus (SY-ruhs) the Great. He brought together the two kingdoms of Medes (MEED-uhs) and Persia. Cyrus took over many lands, including Babylonia. He promised not to destroy the city of Babylon. He respected their religion and culture. The Persians allowed the people

◄ The Jewish people return to Jerusalem.

they took over to keep their religions. Cyrus even repaired Babylonian temples.

Nebuchadnezzar II (neb-yuh-kuh-DREZ-zuhr), a Babylonian ruler, had taken the Hebrews as slaves. In 539 B.C., Cyrus allowed the Hebrews to return to Jerusalem. Cyrus also rebuilt the Hebrew temple in Jerusalem.

The Persian religion taught that there was good and evil in the world. Good people would go to heaven. This belief influenced their politics. Alexander the Great from Greece eventually defeated Persia.

Persia Today

Religion still plays an important part in the governments of the Middle East.

Farsi

The modern Persian language is called Farsi (FAWR-see). Are there any students in your school who speak Farsi?

The Cyrus Cylinder

The Cyrus Cylinder was a written message. It was from Cyrus the Great to Babylonia. He promised not to destroy their city. It was written in cuneiform. The cylinder is found in the British Museum today.

Cyrus ► Cylinder

◄ Ruins at Persepolis

THE HEBREWS

The Hebrews lived on the edge of Mesopotamia. Their civilization was located between Egypt and Assyria on the Mediterranean (MED-uh-tuhr-RAY-nee-uhn) Sea. They were shepherds, farmers, fishermen, and **nomads**.

The father of their religion, Abraham, came from Mesopotamia. Their religion was different from other Mesopotamian cultures. They believed in only one God. Their beliefs taught them that they were chosen by God and had to obey his **commandments**.

◀ This is a Jewish man in Israel.

▲ Hebrew-English Bible

The story of the Hebrews is told in the first five books of the Bible. There was a great **famine** (FAM-uhn). So, the Hebrews went to Egypt for food. There were so many Hebrews coming into Egypt that the pharaoh began to worry they would take over. To keep control over them, he made them slaves. After many years, they escaped from Egypt.

Immigration Today

People from all over the world have immigrated to America. People immigrate for many different reasons. Some of the reasons are the same as the ancient Hebrews. Some people want religious freedom. Others are having famines in their own countries. Or, they are looking for better jobs.

What's in a Name?

The Hebrews are also known as the Israelites (IZ-ree-uhl-ites). They settled in the area known today as Israel (IZ-ree-uhl). Today, many Jewish people trace their roots to the ancient Hebrews.

Sidon
Damascus
PHOENICIA
Tyre
GALILEE
Beth-shan
Samaria
PHILISTIA   Aphek
Ashdod
Cath
Ashkelon   Jerusalem
Gaza
Hebron   MOAB
AMMAN
DEAD SEA
EDOM   DESERT
SINAI DESERT
Elat
GULF OF ACABA

	Empire Under David and Solomon
	Israel 733 B.C.
	Judah 733 B.C.

THE GIFT OF THE ARAMEANS

Another group of people who lived in and around Mesopotamia were the Arameans (air-uh-MEE-uhz). They did not have an empire or a capital city. They first showed up around 1100 B.C. The Arameans caused some problems for the Assyrian Empire. They took over many cities in Syria, Turkey, and Iraq. Many Arameans moved into Mesopotamia.

The most important gift of the Arameans was their language. They spoke Aramaic (air-uh-MAY-ik). When the Persian Empire began, some Arameans were part of the government. So, many people spoke Aramaic. The Persians decided to make Aramaic their own language. The language spread across the ancient Middle East, from Iran to Egypt. Aramaic is still spoken in some places in the Middle East today.

◀ Aramaic script

Jesus spoke ▶
Aramaic.

Something in Common

Two thousand years ago, the Aramaic language was important to different religions. Many religious books were written in Aramaic. Others, like the Bible, were translated into Aramaic. Jesus and others who lived around him spoke Aramaic.

▼ In deserts like those in the ancient Middle East, camels helped in many important ways.

The Language that Ruled

Many different people used the Aramaic language. Most of these people were not Arameans. After Aramaic became the main language of the Persian Empire, the language was used wherever the Persians ruled.

TALENTED PHOENICIANS

The Phoenicians (fih-NEE-shuhnz) were another civilization in the Middle East. They lived in what is now Lebanon (LEB-uh-nawn).

The location and the skills of the Phoenicians made it a great trade center. They built strong ships. And, they had items that other people wanted. The Phoenicians had cedar and pine forests. Wood was rare and highly prized in the desert. The Phoenicians also made a purple dye from a special snail. This color was important to royalty. Phoenicians were the first to make blown glass.

The peak of the Phoenician culture was around 1000 B.C. They were trading with many other places in Italy, Africa, and Spain. In 576 B.C., the Assyrians took over the Phoenicians. The Phoenician culture declined after this.

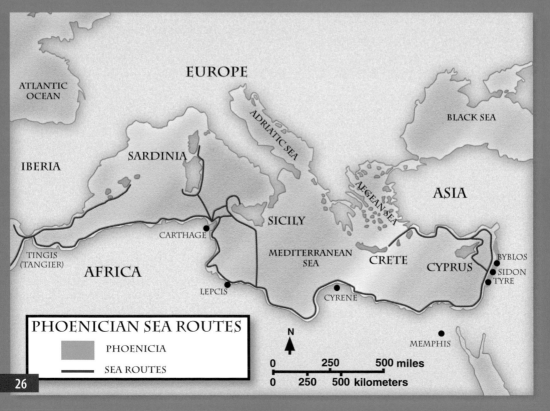

PHOENICIAN SEA ROUTES

PHOENICIA

SEA ROUTES

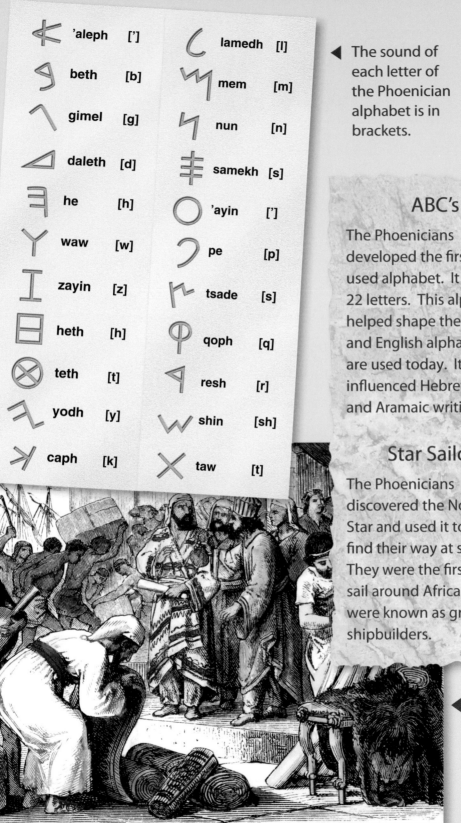

'aleph	[']	lamedh	[l]	
beth	[b]	mem	[m]	
gimel	[g]	nun	[n]	
daleth	[d]	samekh	[s]	
he	[h]	'ayin	[']	
waw	[w]	pe	[p]	
zayin	[z]	tsade	[s]	
heth	[h]	qoph	[q]	
teth	[t]	resh	[r]	
yodh	[y]	shin	[sh]	
caph	[k]	taw	[t]	

◀ The sound of each letter of the Phoenician alphabet is in brackets.

ABC's

The Phoenicians developed the first widely used alphabet. It had 22 letters. This alphabet helped shape the Greek and English alphabets that are used today. It also influenced Hebrew, Arabic, and Aramaic writing.

Star Sailors

The Phoenicians discovered the North Star and used it to help find their way at sea. They were the first to sail around Africa. They were known as great shipbuilders.

◀ Phoenician traders

27

WHY DO I NEED TO KNOW THIS?

Although the ancient civilizations existed thousands of years ago, they still influence people's lives today. The Sumerians created written language and the number system. Sumerians also gave us the wheel and showed us how to use irrigation and flood control. The Babylonians had a strong organized system of government. The Assyrians improved mathematical concepts. The Phoenicians had the first alphabet and used **navigation** (nav-uh-GAY-shuhn).

These ancient civilizations also created many great works of art. And, these amazing people developed the beginnings of great architecture.

The region of Mesopotamia today is still a lively and complicated area. Many people with different religions and cultures live there. There are many conflicts, but there is also hope for peace.

▲ These lions are on the Ishtar Gate in Babylon.

▲ This relief shows Sumerian gods.

◀ An Assyrian sculpture

GLOSSARY

astronomy—the study of the stars

canals—artificial waterways

city-state—an ancient city that ruled itself independently

civilizations—societies that have writing and keep track of records

commandments—orders from God, especially one of the Ten Commandments

cuneiform—writing that uses small wedge-shaped characters

famine—a severe shortage of food resulting in widespread hunger

irrigation—moving water to help crops grow

levees—natural or human-made walls built along rivers to prevent flooding

navigation—directing of the course of a ship

nomads—people who move from place to place to live

scribes—men who wrote in cuneiform

silt—fine-grained sediment at the bottom of a river or lake

societies—a group or community with common interests

stylus—a special writing instrument used for writing on clay tablets

ziggurats—pyramid-like temples

INDEX

IMAGE CREDITS